HOW FAR IS A STAR?

A Question of Science Book

HOW FAR IS A STAR?

by Sidney Rosen
illustrated by Dean Lindberg

 Carolrhoda Books, Inc. / Minneapolis

Each word that appears in **BOLD** in the text is explained in the glossary on page 40.

LIBRARY OF CONGRESS CATALOGING-IN-PUBLICATION DATA

Rosen, Sidney.
  How far is a star? / by Sidney Rosen ; with illustrations by Dean Lindberg.
     p.   cm.—(A Question of science)
  Summary: Explains the vast distances in space and describes different types of stars in the universe using a question-and-answer format.
  ISBN 0-87614-684-1 (lib. bdg.)
  1. Cosmological distances—Juvenile literature. 2. Stars—Miscellanea—Juvenile literature. 3. Astronomy—Miscellanea—Juvenile literature. [1. Stars—Miscellanea. 2. Astronomy—Miscellanea. 3. Questions and answers.]
I. Lindberg, Dean, ill. II. Title. III. Series.
QB991.C66R67   1992
523.8—dc20   91-16107
                                                        CIP
                                                         AC

Manufactured in the United States of America

1 2 3 4 5 6 7 8 9 10 01 00 99 98 97 96 95 94 93 92

How far is a star?

Which star do you mean? The stars we see at night?
Or the star we see during the day?

During the daytime? What star is that?

The star that shines every day and makes life possible
here on Earth—the Sun!

Then the Sun is like a star?

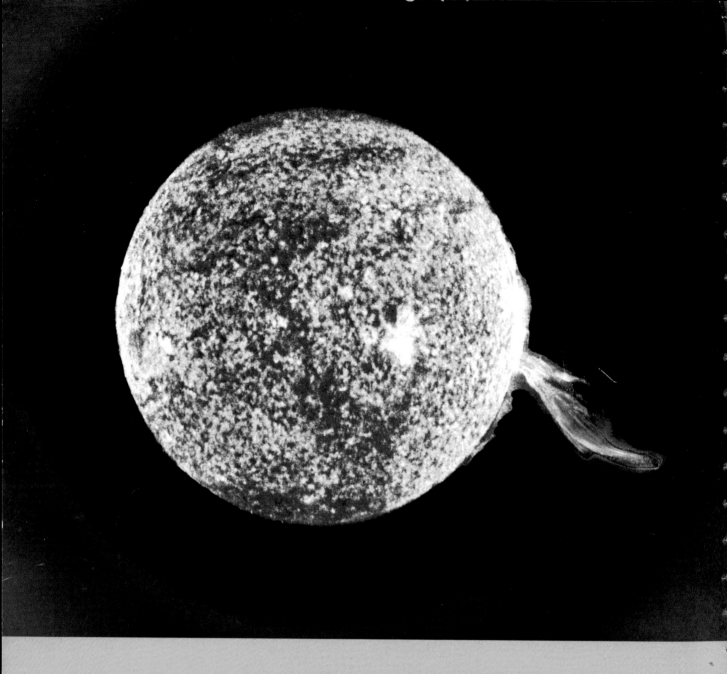

Right. The Sun *is* a star. Like every other star in the sky, the Sun is a burning ball of gas. The Sun's light reaches us here on Earth. It shines on Mercury, Venus, Mars, Jupiter, Saturn, Uranus, Neptune, and Pluto, too.

How far away from us is the Sun, anyway?

It's so hot!

Oh, about 93 million miles.

Ninety-three million? How far is that?

So far it's hard to imagine. But try this idea.
Take a basketball, or a ball about that big.
Put it in the middle of your room.
That basketball is the Sun.

Find a ball about the size of a very small pea or a BB.
That will be the Earth. You can use the two balls to
see how far the Earth is from the Sun.

But you will need to go outside. Because you will have to carry the BB over 25 yards from the basketball! That's about a quarter of a football field away!

How long would it take to get to the Sun in a rocket ship?

Our fastest rocket ships travel at 25,000 miles an hour. At that speed, it would take more than five months to get to the Sun. But who wants to go to the Sun, anyway? It's hot enough to burn up a rocket ship. The Sun is hotter than almost anything we know.

If stars are so hot, why would anyone want to visit them?

Is there life on other planets?

Rocket ships have sent back pictures of the other planets in our Solar System, showing that nothing can live there. It looks as if the Earth is the one planet that is just the right distance from the Sun and has everything needed for life. Out of the billions of stars in space there may be some that — like the Sun — are circled by a planet like Earth. And on that planet there may be life as we know it. But until we find a way of getting to the stars, those planets will remain one of the mysteries of outer space.

Well, we might find other planets going around one of the other stars in the sky. We might even find another planet like Earth going around a star like the Sun.

How long would it take to get there?

That depends on which star you pick. Not a single night star is nearly as close to us as the Sun. And some stars are much farther away than others.

Some stars look brighter than others. Are the brighter ones closer to us?

Not always. Stars are hot burning furnaces that give off light and heat. Their brightness depends on how hot and how big they are, not just on how far they are from us. You can think about it this way. What's brighter, a candle or a hundred-watt light bulb?

Oh, the bulb is much brighter.

That's right. Now suppose the candle is in your room, next to your bed. Look out the window. Down the street, maybe a block away, a hundred-watt bulb is burning in someone's house. You can see the bulb's light shining through a window. Which will look brighter to you, the candle or the bulb?

I'll bet on the candle.

And you'd be right. But the bulb still gives off a brighter light. We see stars—bright ones and dim ones— because their light travels through space to our eyes. Starlight, like the light of a lamp, grows dimmer and dimmer as it travels through space.

But you still haven't answered the question. How long will it take to get to a star?

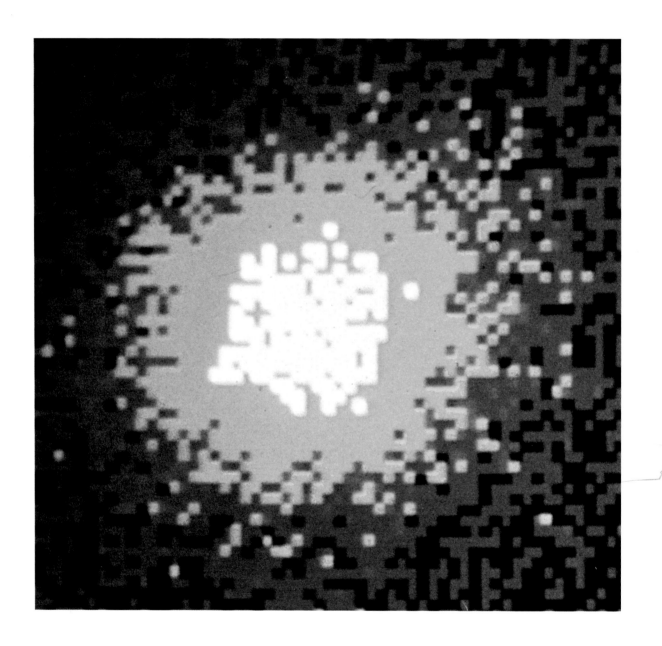

Okay, let's find out. The star that's nearest to us
is one of a group of three stars called Alpha Centauri.
The nearest of the three is Proxima Centauri.

How far away from us is Proxima Centauri?

The universe is enormous. So it isn't practical to measure the distance to the stars in miles. Try this and see. Imagine a measurement called a *snerg*. Let's say that one *snerg* is the smallest distance between the tiniest marks on your ruler. Now, take your ruler and measure the distance around the world in *snergs*. Ridiculous? Well, that's what it would be like to measure the distance to the stars in miles.

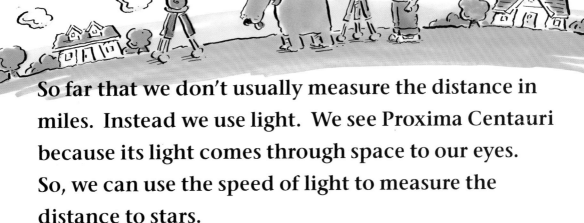

So far that we don't usually measure the distance in miles. Instead we use light. We see Proxima Centauri because its light comes through space to our eyes. So, we can use the speed of light to measure the distance to stars.

How fast does light move?

Light's the fastest moving thing we know.
In one second, light travels about 186,000 miles.
The Sun's light takes only eight minutes to get here.
But it takes Proxima Centauri's light over four years
to travel to Earth.

*Four years at the speed of light! That's a lot of
miles, isn't it?*

On the chalkboard:

186,000
× 60
——————
11,160,000
× 60
——————
669,600,000
× 24
——————
16,070,400,000
× 365
——————
5,865,696,000,000

In the note on the board:

How is a light-year different from a regular year?

A regular year is a measure of *time*. But a light-year is a measure of *distance*, the distance a beam of light will travel in one year. Light travels at about 186,000 miles per second. There are 60 seconds in a minute, 60 minutes in an hour, 24 hours in a day, and 365 days in a year. Do some quick math, and you'll see that light travels almost six *trillion* miles in one year.

You bet! Add it all up, and the nearest star is about 25 trillion miles away. Written out, that's 25,000,000,000,000 miles.

How can anyone imagine a number that big?

It's almost impossible. But we can use the basketball and the BB again. This time, put the smaller ball in the center of your room. That's the Earth. Let the basketball be Proxima Centauri.

How far away will I have to take the basketball?

About 70,000 football fields, or 4,000 miles,
away from the BB!

Is there much chance of my getting to a star then?

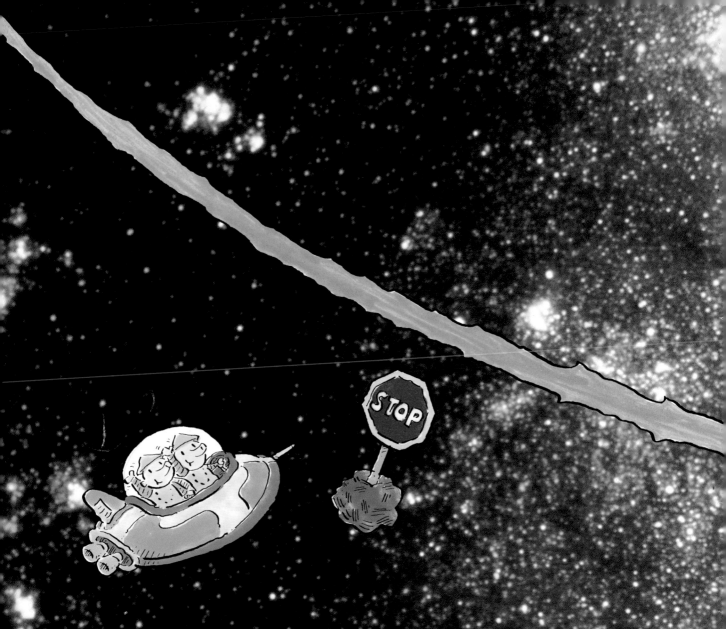

Not yet. Traveling at 25,000 miles an hour and more,
it took a rocket ship 12 years just to get from Earth to
the planet Neptune and the edge of our **Solar System.**
That's pretty slow compared to the speed of light.

*What if I had a rocket ship that could travel at
the speed of light?*

Then you might see some amazing things. You might
see other planets like Earth. And you would certainly
see bright stars, dim stars, red stars, and white stars.

Why so many different kinds of stars?

Just like human beings, stars are born in different sizes. They live through different lifetimes before they burn out.

The colors around the red giant Betelgeuse are made of gas.

How long does it take a star to burn out?

The life of a star has to be counted, not just in years, but in *billions* of years. As the gas in a star slowly burns up, the star changes. As the star's fire burns lower and lower, the star can get fatter and fatter. At the same time, its light becomes redder and redder. It becomes a **red giant**, like the star Betelgeuse.

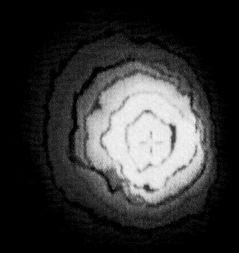

What happens next?

An average-sized star like the Sun will begin to fall in on itself. As the star crushes together, it becomes smaller and smaller. Imagine a house that is getting older and older. Pretty soon the ceilings fall in, then the walls fall in. What was once a large, proud house becomes a small pile of bricks and wood.

How small can a star like that get?

Almost a hundred times smaller than it was! Picture
the Sun crushing in from all sides until it is only about
as big as the Earth—the basketball becomes the BB! The
Sun would burn hotter and hotter, until it was glowing
white-hot. We call that kind of star a **white dwarf**.

Does a white dwarf star stay that way forever?

No. In time, all the fuel burns out and the star dies. It becomes a star that we can't see anymore— a **black dwarf**.

Do all stars become dwarfs or giants?

What will happen to the Sun when it grows old?

It will probably become a red giant. That means it will grow larger and larger and burn with red light. The Sun may even grow big enough to burn up the four planets closest to it — including the Earth. But that won't happen for five billion years or so. Fortunately, five billion years is a *very, very* long time.

No, not if the star is much bigger than the Sun. Then the balance between the inner parts and the outer parts of the star can be upset. Energy grows until the star blows up, like a big firecracker. Bits and pieces of the star fly into space, and that may be the end of that star. But before the star dies, it shines very brightly. Long ago, people saw a very bright star shining where no star had been before.

They thought the star was new and called it "nova," or "new" in Latin. The name stuck, even though the star wasn't new at all. It was a large, older star that had just blown up—what astronomers call **supernovas**. When a star shines very brightly but *doesn't* blow up altogether, it's called a **nova**. Some stars are novas more than once in their lifetimes.

This is leftover dust and gas from a supernova that exploded hundreds of years ago.

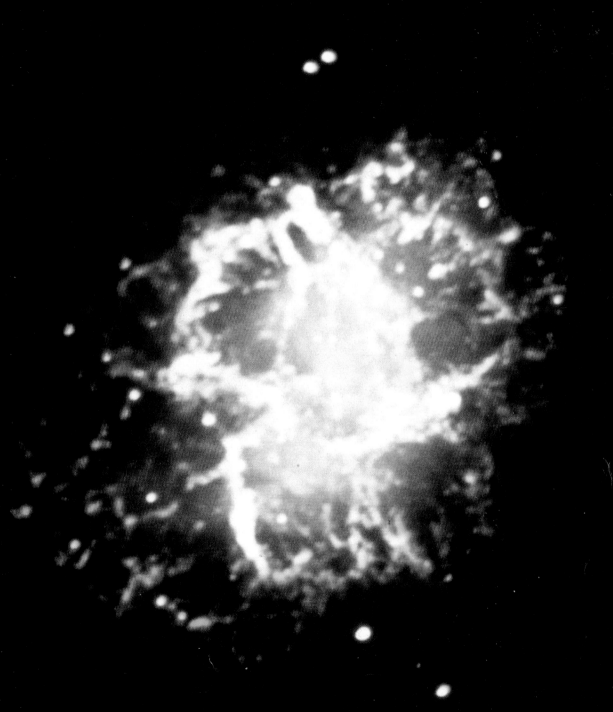

Do novas and supernovas happen very often?

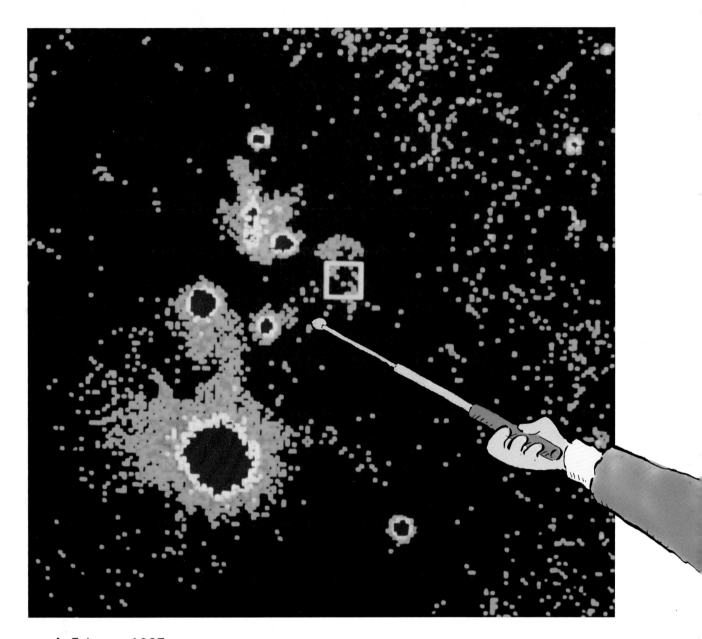

In February 1987, a supernova was
spotted in the Large Magellanic
Cloud, a galaxy outside the Milky Way.
Astronomers call this supernova
1987A. It is visible in the southern
hemisphere, from places like Australia
and South America.

We may not see them all, but two or three dozen stars become novas every year in the Milky Way, our **galaxy**. Supernovas don't happen as often. During the past one thousand years, people have seen only six of them in the Milky Way.

What else can happen to a star?

Extra-large stars can fall in on themselves and
change in amazing ways. Imagine that a giant hand
is squeezing an extra-large star. The star is squeezed
smaller and smaller until it's only a few miles across.
This small star pulls things toward it. Its pull is so
great that even light can't get away from the star.
We call that kind of star a **black hole**.

Could the Sun become a black hole?

How can you tell if you've found a black hole?

I can't find my shoes!

Maybe they got sucked into a Black Hole!

Astronomers believe that certain stars become black holes in space, but so far they haven't found any. It's hard to find black holes, because we can't see them the way we can see other stars. **Gravity**, the same force that squashes the star smaller and smaller, keeps light from leaving a black hole. So, there's no light to come through a telescope to our eyes. It's possible that some black holes do have **X rays** coming from them. Even though we can't see X rays, we can photograph them. Maybe that's the way we'll finally find a star that's a black hole.

On the occasion of my 5 billionth Birthday, I'd like my friends to know I'm in good health and looking forward to my next 5 billion years!

No, the Sun would have to be a much bigger star to turn into a black hole. We don't have to worry about the Sun. It's five billion years old now, just middle-aged. The Sun won't be really old until another five billion years have passed.

That's a relief. Will we ever reach the stars?

GLOSSARY

black dwarf: All that's left when the fuel of a white dwarf star has burned out and cooled off

black hole: A collapsed star whose gravity is so strong that nothing, not even light, can escape from the star

galaxy: A great collection of millions or billions of stars, gas, and dust held together by gravity. The Milky Way is *our* galaxy.

gravity: The force that makes objects attract each other. The Earth's gravity is so strong it keeps us stuck to Earth.

light-year: The distance a beam of light travels in one year, about six trillion miles

nova: A star that gives out a sudden burst of energy, so it shines far more brightly for a while

red giant: A large star that is bright, but getting cooler. Its lower temperature makes the star look red.

Solar System: The Sun and all the bodies that move around it—planets, moons, comets, asteroids, and meteors

supernova: An extra-great explosion of a star that causes the star, in just a few days, to shine millions of times brighter than usual

white dwarf: A star about the size of the Sun whose fuel has burned up. The star has become much, much smaller in size, and the leftover heat makes the star white-hot.

X rays: High-energy, invisible light that can go through certain materials. Some stars send out this form of light.